REDBACK publishing

AUSTRALIAN TRANSPORT

ROAD TRANSPORT

ALISON HIDEKI

First Published 2018 by
Redback Publishing
Suite 6, 13a Narabang Way,
Belrose NSW 2085
Australia

www.redbackpublishing.com
orders@redbackpublishing.com

ISBN 978-1-761401-55-8

Author: Alison Hideki
Editor: Marianne Lindsell
Designer: Redback Publishing

Original illustrations © Redback Publishing 2025
Originated by Redback Publishing

Acknowledgements
Abbreviations: l—left, r—right, b—bottom, t—top, c—centre, m—middle
We would like to thank the following for permission to reproduce photographs: (Images © shutterstock)
p10r by Arthur Phillip Contributed By State Records New South Wales [CGS 13859, [SZ430]],
p6b Section of Great North Road by Conollyb via wikimedia, p7r Convict built stone embankment by Stephen Gard via Wikimedia Commons.

Every effort has been made to contact copyright holders of any material reproduced in this book. Any omissions will be rectified in subsequent printings if notice is given to the publisher.

A catalogue record for this book is available from the National Library of Australia

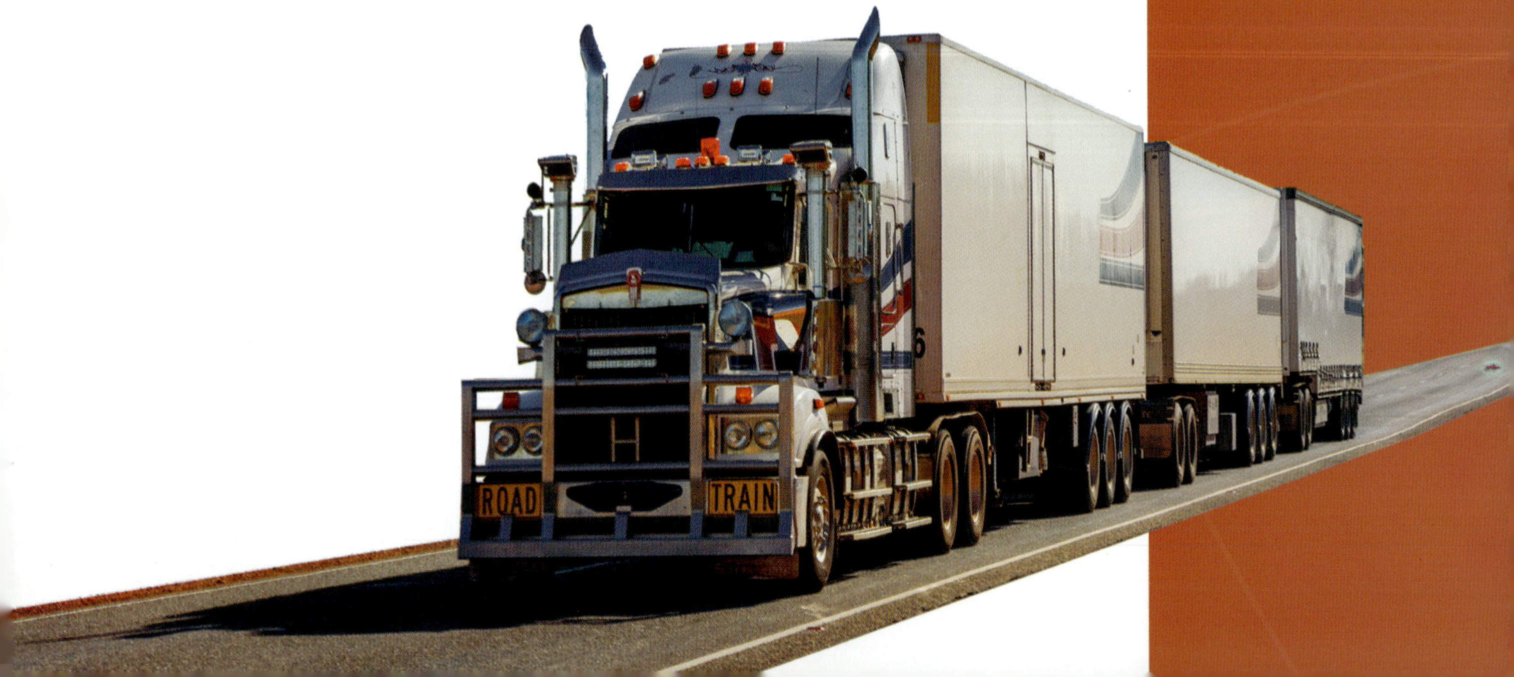

CONTENTS

ON THE ROAD

Millions of Australians use roads every day.
More people use road transport than any other type of transport.

ROADS IN AUSTRALIA

There are more than 917,000 kilometres of roads in Australia. Cars, buses, trucks, vans, semi-trailers, motorcycles and bicycles transport people and goods on all sorts of Australian roads, from eight-lane freeways in cities to rough dirt tracks in remote parts of the outback. There are sealed (tarred) roads right around the continent and through the outback from Adelaide to Darwin.

NORTHERN AUSTRALIA ROADS PROGRAMME

In 2016, the Australian Government announced the Northern Australia Roads Programme that will help improve Northern Australia's transport and road network.

Road traffic is a major cause of air pollution in Australian cities

VEHICLES AND DRIVERS

There are more than 18.4 million registered motor vehicles in Australia. More than 80 per cent of Australians over 16 years of age hold a drivers licence.

More than 500,000 registered trucks use Australian roads. Shops and factories rely on vans, trucks and semi-trailers to deliver and receive goods, and mail is carried between towns by truck. Trucks travel around 17,000 million kilometres each year.

TRANSPORT

Transport is the movement of people or goods from one place to another. There are many kinds of transport, including airplanes, cars, trucks, ships, trains, pipelines and conveyor belts. Transport has always been very important for humans, as it makes it possible for people to communicate with one another, and to trade with one another.

THE FIRST ROADS

Australian people have travelled overland for many thousands of years. Aboriginal nations traded with each other. Traders travelled hundreds of kilometres along paths that were not always marked, but were remembered and passed on from generation to generation. Aboriginal people had no need for roads. Roads as we know them today were not built until after the arrival of Europeans in 1788.

Convicts built the Great North Road, north of Sydney, in 1829-30.

EARLY ROADS

The first roads in Australia were built in Sydney from 1788. The first bridge was built across a creek called the Tank Stream. In 1794, the first major road was cleared. It stretched from Sydney to Parramatta and on to Windsor. It was used by people walking, riding horses and travelling in horse-drawn and bullock-drawn wagons.

In 1814, convicts built a road across the Blue Mountains, west of Sydney. This opened up the western plains for European farmers. Soon people were driving herds of cattle along the road or transporting their belongings in horse-drawn carts.

In Tasmania, a road from Hobart to Launceston was built in 1818. In 1825, a bridge was built near Richmond, Tasmania. It is the oldest existing bridge in Australia. In 1835, a track linking Sydney and Melbourne was completed.

Tank Stream

CONVICT BUILDERS

Most early roads were built by gangs of convicts. They cut trees to clear the paths for the roads, and built stone walls and drainage channels to stop the road surfaces from being washed away. The roads were built from rocks and gravel.

One of the best examples of a convict-built road is the Great North Road, in Dharug National Park, north of Sydney. It was built in 1829-30, and has stone walls of up to 12 metres in height. The road was the main link between Sydney and Newcastle. It was used only for about 50 years before being replaced by a road further to the west.

Convict built wall along the Great North Road

THE FIRST VEHICLES

COBB AND CO

The Cobb and Co coach company was formed by an American, Freeman Cobb, in Melbourne in 1853. By 1870, Cobb and Co horse-drawn coaches carried mail, freight and passengers over 11,000 kilometres of roads, from South Australia to northern Queensland. The company used 6,000 horses every day.

ANIMAL POWER

During the 1800s, goods were carried overland by horse-drawn or bullock-drawn wagons. In outback areas, camels carried people and goods. Bullock drays were the most common method of moving heavy loads overland. They were used to transport wool from inland sheep stations to ports on rivers or on the coast. Bullock drays were driven by 'bullockies', who walked alongside the bullocks, cracking whips to keep them moving.

BICYCLES

Bicycles became popular after the 1880s. At first they were 'pennyfarthing' bicycles, which were very hard to ride. Later bicycles were better designed, which led to bicycles becoming a popular way of travelling in towns and cities.

PETROL-ENGINE CARS

The first petrol-engine cars were brought to Australia in 1900. In 1904, Australia's first car race was held at Sandown Park, near Melbourne. Harley Tarrant won it in a car he had built himself. In 1905, a 'reliability trial' was run from Melbourne to Sydney and back. The winner covered about 2,000 kilometres in 50 hours, averaging about 40 kilometres per hour.

STEAM CARS

The first car built in Australia was made by David and John Shearer at Mannum, South Australia, in 1896. It had a steam engine. In 1900, Herbert Thomson and Edward Holmes drove a steam car from Bathurst, New South Wales, to Melbourne. It took them 10 days to travel 800 kilometres. They became bogged many times, and had several accidents.

ROAD TRANSPORT IN CITIES

When Governor Arthur Phillip landed in Sydney Cove in 1788, one of the first things he did was draw up a plan of where the roads of the new town would run. However, his plan was ignored by settlers, soldiers and convicts, who built their houses where they pleased. Boggy rutted tracks developed in the spaces between the buildings. The streets of central Sydney today mostly follow these original tracks.

Plan of the streets of the town of Sydney 1832

Other cities such as Melbourne and Adelaide were planned on a grid system, which was followed by the people when they built houses and shops.

Road traffic needs to be controlled to make sure it flows and to keep the number of accidents low. Road rules, road markings, signs and signals help to control traffic.

EARLY CITY ROADS

At first, city roads were used mainly by pedestrians and horse riders. Wagons, carriages and bullock drays also used the roads, causing them to become boggy in wet weather and dusty in dry weather. Dung from the animals covered the roads, making pedestrians very careful where they put their feet! Water troughs were provided for the animals, and in some towns 'hitching rails' provided places for horses to be tied up.

EARLY ROAD SURFACES

In the early days, sawdust and woodchips were strewn over the roads, and gutters were built to drain rainwater. Wooden blocks were also used, as well as cobblestones (that covered the road with closely packed stones). In 1848, the first 'macadamised' road was built in Heidelberg Road, Melbourne. A macadamised road is made with an earth foundation covered by a layer of crushed rock, which is rolled flat. Later asphalt was added to keep the rock layer solid, and to stop it being washed away. Bridges across creeks and rivers were made of stone or wood.

CITY ROADS TODAY

Congestion in Australia's capital cities has become so bad that the annual cost of delays caused by workers being stuck in traffic has been estimated to be in the billions of dollars, and rising each year.

A 2017 report states that Sydney motorists endure seven of the ten worst roads in the country, with Pennant Hills Road between Parramatta and Hornsby having the worst delays and economic toll in the country.

The other three worst roads for congestion are in Melbourne.

URBAN SPRAWL

The spread of roads and the increased use of cars meant houses could be built further from where people shopped and worked. After 1950, large cities such as Brisbane, Sydney and Melbourne spread into the farmlands around them. Traditional kinds of public transport such as trains were less popular, as many houses were built a long way from railway lines.

Cars became the most popular way to travel in cites, and roads had to be improved. Freeways were built, and extra lanes were added to main roads.

CONTROLLING TRAFFIC

Cars also have signals for safety. Turn indicators (blinkers) show that a vehicle is about to turn or change lanes, and brake lights show when the driver applies the brakes.

Today there is a network of country roads linking towns, cities and remote communities across Australia. Most roads are sealed (tarred), but many are gravel.

WHERE ROADS MEET

Traffic at intersections is controlled with stop signs, give way signs, roundabouts and traffic lights. Signals also stop traffic to allow pedestrians to cross busy roads.

Many city streets have a speed limit of 50 kilometres an hour.

KEEP TRAFFIC MOVING

Cars use more fuel and emit more polluting gases when they start moving than they do when travelling at even speeds. Traffic controllers try to find ways of keeping traffic moving without frequent stopping and starting.

Freeways have been built in some places. These roads either go over or under the roads that cross them so that the freeway traffic doesn't have to stop for other cars at intersections. Roads called ramps take traffic on and off the freeways.

On other roads, roundabouts at busy intersections can help to keep traffic moving. Cars don't have to stop unless there is a lot of traffic arriving at the roundabout at the same time. Traffic lights are set so cars travelling on a main road should receive a series of green lights. Cameras monitor busy intersections, and traffic controllers can change the way traffic signals operate to try to clear congested streets.

SLOWING TRAFFIC DOWN

Traffic is slowed on residential streets to make them safer for pedestrians and quieter for residents. Speed humps, oneway street systems and traffic islands that make streets narrower all help to slow traffic.

25

COUNTRY ROADS

Roads have been built across all kinds of landscapes in Australia. In places, bridges and tunnels have been built to cross creeks, rivers and bays as well as mountainous areas.

The Eyre Highway

HIGHWAYS

Major highways link all capital cities. The road from Sydney to Melbourne, the Hume Highway, is mostly four lanes wide, with many sections of freeway. Freeways and major multi-lane highways also link Melbourne and Ballarat, Melbourne and Geelong, Sydney and Wollongong, Sydney and Newcastle, and Brisbane and the Gold Coast.

Adelaide and Perth are linked by the Eyre Highway, which crosses the Nullarbor Plain. The Eyre Highway was sealed in 1976.

The Hume Highway

EARLY COUNTRY ROADS

The first country roads were rough tracks worn by horses' hooves and cartwheels as they followed the same routes over and over again. These roads became muddy bogs after rain, and the wheels of heavy carts left deep ruts that made travelling over them bumpy and uncomfortable. There were few bridges, so creeks were crossed at fords (shallow parts). When cars were brought to Australia in the early 1900s, roads needed to be improved. Proper foundations were laid, and gravel surfaces were graded to keep them flat and to smooth out ruts. Busy roads were sealed, although most country roads remained gravel until after 1950.

HIGHWAY ONE

After World War II, the Australian Government decided that an all weather road should be built around Australia. This road was named National Highway One. In 1974 the Federal Government decided that the entire road should be sealed. The job was finally completed in December 1989 when the section between Newman and Port Hedland (Western Australia) was finished.

DEFENCE NEEDS

World War II brought a change to road construction, especially in the outback. Troops needed to be moved quickly from place to place, so more roads were built. A road was built for military vehicles between Mount Isa and Tennant Creek in 1941. This meant that cars could travel directly between Brisbane and Darwin.

MAKING ROADS, BRIDGES, AND TUNNELS

Most Australians use road transport every day. They may travel to work and school by car or bus, or drive to shops or to visit friends or relatives. People may also travel from one town to another using a highway.

MODERN ROADS

Different road surfaces are used depending on the type of ground they are built on and the amount of traffic they will carry. The most common type of road surface is bitumen, which is crushed rock (often called 'blue metal') held together with asphalt. Asphalt is made from petroleum oil, and is produced when petrol is made. A bitumen surface is strong, but it is also flexible and will bend slightly under heavy loads without cracking.

As bitumen roads age, they crumble and need frequent mending. Maintenance teams patch potholes and mend road edges that have started to break away.

Some busy freeways are made from concrete, laid over compressed crushed rock. This type of road often has a steel grid set into the concrete to make the road even stronger. The concrete surface is usually 15-45 centimetres thick.

Asphalt road surface on top of layers of crushed rock

SYDNEY HARBOUR BRIDGE

The Sydney Harbour Bridge was built between 1924 and 1932. When it was finished it was the longest steel arch bridge in the world. The arch has a span of 503 metres, and the entire bridge covers a length of more than one kilometre. The top of the arch is about 135 metres above water level. The deck, which is 50 metres wide, carries eight lanes of traffic, two railway lines, a cycleway and a pedestrian path. More than 180,000 vehicles cross the bridge every day.

MAKING BRIDGES

Bridges in the past were made from stone or wood. After 1900, steel and concrete were used to make larger, stronger bridges. As roads were built to new destinations, bridges were built over freeways and railway lines.

TUNNELS

There are fewer road tunnels built in Australia than in many other nations, mainly because Australia has fewer high mountains. The longest road tunnel in Australia is Brisbane's Airport Link, at 6.7 kilometres.

LONG BRIDGES

The Macleay Valley Bridge over the Macleay River is the longest bridge in Australia. It is located along the Pacific Highway. Before it opened, the Ted Smout Memorial Bridge in Brisbane was the country's longest bridge.

The Westgate Bridge in Melbourne is 2.6 kilometres long, and is Australia's third longest bridge. Construction commenced in 1968, and the bridge was opened in November 1978. Tragedy struck in 1970 when a section of the partly completed bridge collapsed, killing 35 workers.

ROAD FREIGHT

Road vehicles carry most goods that are transported between towns and cities in Australia. Road vehicles also make most deliveries to factories and shops.

DELIVERY VANS AND TRUCKS

In towns and cities, vans and small trucks deliver goods to shops and factories. Trucks are also used in country areas to transport animals and farm supplies. Removalists move people's belongings from one house to another in trucks called removal vans.

SEMI-TRAILERS

Most heavy trucks are semi-trailers. Semi-trailers are powerful trucks that pull one large trailer. The trailer may carry a container that has been brought to Australia by ship, or general goods packed into a large trailer or loaded on to a flat tray and covered with a tarpaulin. Special trailers are made to transport petrol, coal, wheat and chemicals. Refrigerated trailers are used to transport foods such as milk, meat and vegetables that may spoil if they become warm.

ROAD TRAINS

In country areas, road trains carry goods. These are like semi-trailers, but have several trailers instead of one. They are often used to transport cattle and sheep, but are also used to transport goods to large inland towns such as Alice Springs and Mount Isa. Triple road trains (with three trailers) may be more than 50 metres long. Road trains have to be marked with signs, and are only allowed on some roads.

ADVANTAGES OF ROAD TRANSPORT

Road transport has an advantage over other types of transport because roads link most destinations in Australia. Goods only have to be loaded and unloaded once because trucks can drive directly to where the goods are to be delivered. Goods transported by rail, sea or air usually have to be taken to the rail terminal, port or airport by road, loaded on to the plane or ship, and then unloaded at the other end for transport by road to the final destination. In most cases, this makes road transport cheaper and faster than sea or rail transport. Air transport is usually faster than road transport, but is much more expensive.

PASSENGER TRANSPORT

Many people work in the road transport industry. They are employed by locals and State Governments, the Federal Government and by private companies.

Roads and vehicles will be improved over the next 50 years to make road transport safer and less damaging to the environment.

MODERN CARS

Modern cars are safer and use less fuel than older cars. Cars today are designed to 'crumple' when they hit something. This increases the amount of damage to the vehicle, but slows it more gradually so the passengers are usually not as badly injured as they might have been. Safety features such as seatbelts and airbags have also greatly reduced the number of people killed and seriously injured in car accidents. Cars today are quieter and more comfortable than older cars. They have better suspension, which means passengers are not jolted as much by bumps, and cars do not lean as much when they go around bends.

PUBLIC TRANSPORT AND PRIVATE TRANSPORT

Public transport is transport provided for all people to use, usually for a fare. Buses and taxis are used to provide public transport on roads. Cars owned and used by individual people are known as private vehicles. Many people prefer to use public transport whenever they can, so that air pollution and traffic congestion can be reduced. Buses carry large numbers of people in one vehicle. They use less fuel and take up less road space than the cars that would be needed to carry the same numbers of people. However, public transport is only available over certain routes. Many people find that there is no direct bus route from their homes to their workplaces. They can use their own cars to travel there more quickly and easily.

LONG DISTANCE TRAVEL

People travel long distances either in private cars, or aboard buses. Coach companies run regular services between towns and cities, and coaches have replaced train services in many areas. Groups such as sporting teams and school children also use coaches for long distance travel. Passengers travel long distances much faster than in the past because roads and vehicles are both better made, which also makes travel today safer.

Buses are an important form of public transport in Australian cities.

FUELLING ROAD TRANSPORT

Cars, trucks and buses run on fuel made from petroleum. Petroleum (also known as crude oil or petroleum oil) is obtained from oil wells drilled deep beneath the Earth's surface. It formed from the remains of sea creatures that sank to the bottom of seas and oceans millions of years ago. The remains of the creatures broke down, forming a thick, oily black liquid. Oil deposits formed when a layer of rock trapped the oil.

Australia produces some petroleum from wells in Bass Strait and off the northwest coast of Western Australia. Supplies are also imported from the Middle East.

PETROL, DIESEL AND LPG

The most common form of fuel used for road transport is petrol. It is bought at service stations. Most petrol sold in Australia is unleaded. In the past lead was added to make the petrol burn more evenly in the engine. When it was found that the lead caused dangerous air pollution, new car engines were modified and unleaded petrol was introduced.

Diesel fuel is a heavier fuel than petrol. It is used mainly by trucks and buses, but also becoming more popular for cars. Diesel is cheaper to produce than petrol and now used by 21 per cent of vehicles in Australia.

Another type of fuel used in some cars is LPG (Liquefied Petroleum Gas). It is made from natural gas, which is a gas that is trapped in rock like crude oil. Natural gas is put under high pressure so it becomes a liquid. In cars, LPG is kept in special high-pressure gas tanks.

PRODUCTS OF PETROLEUM

Petroleum is distilled (heated until part of it turns into a gas, which is collected and then cooled to become a liquid) to make petrol and other products. Other products made from distilling petroleum include kerosene, diesel, aircraft fuel (avgas), grease and bitumen (used to make roads). Petrochemicals, which are used to make plastics, are also produced.

ROAD SAFETY

The number of cars on Australian roads increased sharply after 1950. The number of road accidents also increased. By the 1960s, governments had to find ways to reduce the number of deaths and injuries caused by traffic accidents. Today, Australia's road toll has been cut to less than half what it was in 1970, but still about 1,200 people are killed in road accidents every year.

SEATBELTS AND AIRBAGS

Until the 1970s, very few cars were fitted with seatbelts. In 1971, most State Governments made the wearing of seatbelts compulsory. All new cars from that time had to have seatbelts fitted. The road toll started to fall at this time because people restrained by seatbelts were more likely to survive car accidents.

During the 1990s, many new cars were fitted with airbags, which prevented serious head injuries to many drivers and front-seat passengers involved in car accidents.

The airbag module is designed to inflate extremely rapidly then quickly deflate during impact

IMPROVED ROAD SIGNS, WARNING SIGNS AND ROAD SAFETY DEVICES

Better roads have also improved road safety. Roundabouts and traffic lights at busy intersections help to prevent collisions. Turning lanes give cars space to slow down to turn at intersections without slowing the other traffic. Road signs warn about hazards ahead, such as sharp bends or roadworks.

RADARS AND CAMERAS

Speeding is a major cause of traffic accidents. Speed limits on roads save lives by making sure drivers travel at a speed that is safe for the conditions. Radars and cameras are used to detect and record cars that are breaking the speed limit, and speeding drivers are fined.

CAMPAIGNS AGAINST DRINK DRIVING AND FATIGUE

About a quarter of all drivers killed in traffic accidents have illegal amounts of alcohol in their bloodstreams, and about half of all car accidents are caused by drivers who were drinking alcohol shortly before driving.

Between 1976 and 1982, police in most states began random breath tests. The tests are still used today. Police stop cars at random and give drivers breath tests to detect levels of alcohol in the blood. This has deterred drivers from drinking before they drive, and has also reduced the road toll. For years, advertisements showing the horrors of road accidents due to drink driving have been shown on television.

Fatigue is another killer on Australian roads, with many accidents occurring when drivers fall asleep at the wheel, usually on long trips. Driver fatigue signs remind drivers to take a break, and rest stops often provide refreshment vans during holiday periods.

FAST FACTS

- *In 2016, 34 million random breath tests were performed in NSW*
- *90% of drink drivers in fatal accidents are male*
- *90% of drink driving accidents occur in rural areas*
- *33% of fatal accidents involving drink are in drivers aged 17–24 years*

Speed cameras take photos of cars that are speeding

WORKING ON THE ROADS

Many people work in the road transport industry. They are employed by locals and State Governments, the Federal Government and by private companies.

KEEPING VEHICLES RUNNING

Motor mechanics are employed to service and repair cars, trucks and buses. They are usually employed by garages, motor dealers and companies that own large numbers of vehicles such as bus companies. Motor mechanics are trained on the job while attending a TAFE (Technical and Further Education) course.

DRIVING

Drivers are employed to drive delivery vans, trucks, semi-trailers, road trains, taxis and buses. They must pass a driving test and hold a driver's licence. Drivers of heavy vehicles such as trucks and buses must pass an extra test to allow them to drive those types of vehicles.

MAKING AND REPAIRING ROADS

Roads and bridges are built by governments and by private companies. People are employed as engineers, machinery operators, traffic controllers and labourers. Road patrol workers check the condition of roads, and make minor repairs by filling potholes and re-marking lines. Workers also clean litter from the roadside, and maintain gardens in median strips and roundabouts.

POLICE AND EMERGENCY SERVICES

Police patrol roads to make sure drivers are obeying the road rules. They also operate radar speed cameras and conduct random breath tests. When an accident occurs, police and ambulance services are called. If there has been a fuel spill or if there is any danger of an explosion or a leak of poisonous material, the fire brigade will also attend.

WORKING IN PETROL STATIONS

There are thousands of petrol stations in Australia. Many of them are open all day and night. They are staffed by cashiers and owners or managers who run the businesses and buy fuel from the fuel companies. Tanker drivers deliver fuel to petrol stations.

TRAFFIC OF THE FUTURE

Roads and vehicles will be improved over the next 50 years to make road transport safer and less damaging to the environment.

NEW TECHNOLOGY

Petrol and diesel engines produce large amounts of carbon dioxide, carbon monoxide and other gases that cause air pollution. Scientists have been researching alternative sources of power to help reduce pollution. However, there is another reason to look for an alternative to petrol power. The world's supply of petroleum will run out, so the cars of the future will use alternative power sources. More electric cars and buses are now on the roads. Tech companies are joining forces with car companies to create digital cars of the future.

Electric car recharging

ROAD SAFETY AND TRAFFIC CONGESTION

Great advances have been made in road safety, but in the future, cars will be made even safer as they will be made from stronger materials; braking systems and suspension will be improved; roads will be improved; and safety devices will be fitted in all cars.

There may come a time in the near future when all cars drive themselves and all the passengers have to do is enter the destination and then sit back and enjoy the ride.

TRAFFIC CONTROL

As the number of cars on Australia's roads increases in the future, new measures will be needed to make traffic flow more smoothly and more safely. There might be more lanes reserved for buses, taxis and cars with more than one occupant. More streets may be reserved for use by buses.

GPS technology will make it easier for cars to know when and where there are traffic jams and how to avoid them.

Future self navigating car

FIND OUT MORE

PRIMARY AND SECONDARY SOURCES

A primary source is information created by someone who was a part of or witnessed the historical event first hand. Primary sources are very important to historians researching events and time periods. Examples of primary sources are letters, emails, filmed interviews and clips, journals and diaries, census statistics, government documents, art and maps (from the time period), the news (both print and film), photographs and maps.

A secondary source is when someone who did not actually witness the event retells the facts that someone else told them. Examples of secondary sources include news (both print and film), interviews, letters, journals and diaries, biographies, textbooks and paraphrased quotations.

SEARCH KEY WORDS

Australian roads
country roads
trucks
semi-trailers
tunnels
transport
state roads
road trains
car ownership
bridges

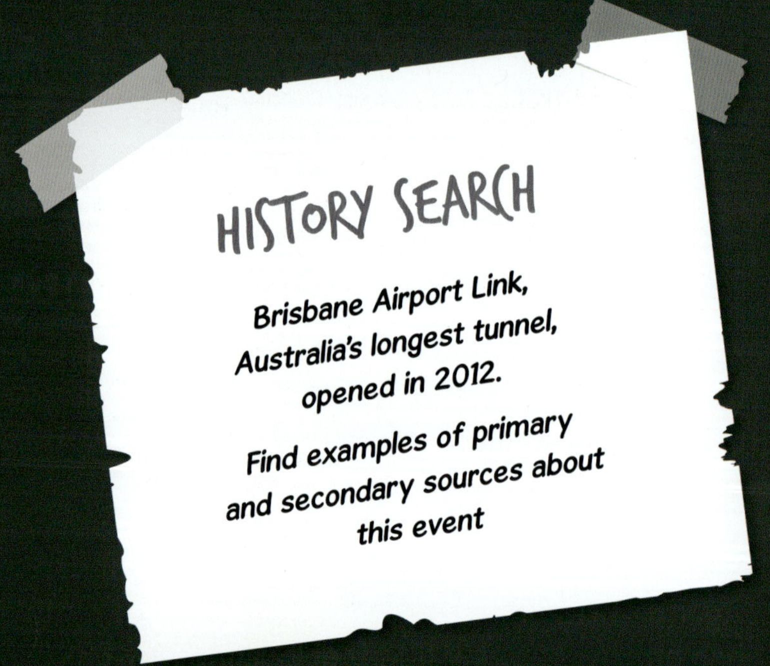

GLOSSARY

Alcohol drinks such as beer and wine. Alcohol can slow your reflex time and impair driving ability

Compulsory required to be done

Convict a person convicted of a crime

Device an implement or machine that does a particular job

Drink driving driving under the influence of alcohol

Freeway a road designed for high speed traffic

Freight goods sent by rail, road, sea or air

Graded made level and even

Highway a major road

Intersection a place where two roads meet

Maintenance keeping in good working order

Road train a powerful truck pulling two or more trailers

Sealed roads roads covered in a hard material such as concrete or bitumen

Semi-trailer a powerful truck pulling a long trailer

INDEX